A TREASURY
OF CLASSIC
MEAT RECIPES

by
Michelle A. Preston

JBG Publishing
Los Angeles
Printed in the United States
All Rights Reserved

TABLE OF CONTENTS

Introduction

7

There's no doubt about it, meat is the King at dinner tables across America—and for good reason. In general, meat contains between 15% and 20% protein. Meat is an excellent source for B-complex vitamins, including vitamin B12, thiamine, niacin, and riboflavin, and meat also contains such important minerals as phosphorous and iron.

In her *A Treasury Of Classic Meat Recipes*, Michelle A. Preston offers delectable recipes for such meats as beef, ham, lamb, pork, variety meats, and veal. Some of these recipes are old classics while others feature some of the latest gourmet twists! Likewise, Mrs. Preston has included recipes that require hardly any effort at all, as well as recipes that will bring out the gourmet cook in you!

Purchasing Meat

Ever since the Meat Inspection Act of 1906, all meat that is bought and sold in interstate commerce must be inspected by government inspectors. Beef, veal and lamb are graded according to the following categories:

Prime: The highest quality of meat sold, prime cuts are usually from young, grain-fed cattle. Prime cuts often appear to be cherry red in color, with small streaks of white fat throughout the cut. These white streaks contribute to the overall tenderness and juiciness of the beef.

Choice: With roughly 75% of all beef earning this rating, choice cuts are the most popular type of meat on the market today; they are also lower in calories than prime cuts. Choice cuts have the same high quality as prime, but contain less excess fat. An excellent purchase when buying fillets, roast beef, and steaks.

Good: Good cuts, while containing less fat (and thus less flavor and tenderness) than choice or prime, are still an excellent buy for the price, especially for pot roasts and stews.

Standard: Because standard cuts come from young animals, they tend to have very little fat, and thus extremely mild flavor. Good for people looking for extremely lean meat.

Commercial: This type of lean cut, primarily from older cattle, is not often found in local supermarkets, but can still provide an economical and tasty dish.

Helpful Buying Tips

Beef should be firm, moist, and odorless (after rinsing) when purchased.

Lamb should be light to dark pink, and lamb fat a creamy pink color.

Pork should appear grayish pink and contain a layer of firm white fat.

Veal should be a light grayish-pink color, with very little fat.

Variety meats and pork are the least expensive meats you can buy.

Buy meat on Thursdays, when butchers and supermarkets have stocked up for the weekend.

Buy beef in the winter, when prices are lower.

BEEF

Seven Blade Roast With East Gravy

3 to 7 pound blade roast
3 onions, quartered
3 celery stalks, cut coarsely
4 carrots, cut coarsely
salt
pepper
Accent (to taste)
1 bay leaf

Gravy:
2 cans golden mushroom soup
2 packages brown gravy mix

1) Fill roasting pan with water to top of roast. Add above ingredients. Cover.

2) Put in oven at 350 degrees for 45 to 50 minutes per pound.

3) 45 minutes prior to roast being done, take out ½ water, celery and carrots. Mix mushroom soup and gravy mix in a bowl. Blend well.

4) Add gravy mixture to roast with remaining water. Place roast back in oven for final 45 minutes, leave uncovered. If necessary, thicken gravy with corn starch.

Serves 4 to 8

Mrs. Soloman J. Cephass
Santa Ana, CA

12

Pop's Hamburger

1½ pounds hamburger
1 teaspoon salt
½ teaspoon pepper
1½ tablespoons onion, grated
1½ tablespoons parsley, minced
½ teaspoon sugar

1) Mix all of the ingredients together. Make 6 hamburger patties. Brown in pan or barbecue and serve.

Serves 6

Traditional Corned Beef and Cabbage

2 pounds lean corned beef
water
½ cabbage, cored and quartered

1) Remove brine from corned beef and place in a pot. Cover with water and boil over a low flame.

2) When water has boiled for 10 minutes, skim off the scum, cover the pot, and simmer for 3 hours or until meat is tender.

3) Remove 2 cups of the cooking liquid and place in a pot with the cabbage. Cook for 15 minutes and serve with the corned beef.

Serves 4

Busy Day Casserole

1 to 1½ pounds lean ground beef
1 medium onion, chopped
1 or 2 cans corn (whole kernel) or whatever
vegetables you like
1 large package frozen hash browns
1 can mushroom pieces
2 cans condensed cream soup (mushroom,
celery or chicken)
1 soup can milk

1) Spray 9 by 13 inch pan with non-stick spray. Put broken up beef in bottom, then add onions, vegetables, mushrooms and hash browns. Thin soup with 1 can milk and pour over top.

2) Bake at 350 degrees for 1 hour or until meat is done. Sprinkle with grated cheddar cheese over top and return to oven until cheese is melted.

Serves 6

Gladys Shutts
Belle Plaine, IA

Flank Steak

3 pounds flank steak, sliced into ¼ inch thick strips
2 medium onions, chopped
4 tablespoons butter
4 tablespoons flour
3 tablespoons vinegar
3 teaspoons dry mustard
1½ teaspoons paprika
¾ teaspoon thyme
1 teaspoon salt
¾ teaspoon cayenne
1½ cups water

1) Saute the onions in 2 tablespoons of butter.

2) Sprinkle the flank steak with 3 tablespoons flour, and add them to the onions, cooking rapidly for 5 minutes on each side.

3) Add 2 tablespoons butter to the same pan and stir in 1 tablespoon of flour and the remaining ingredients. Simmer for 3 to 5 minutes and pour over the flank steak.

Serves 6

Traditional Brisket

3 pound brisket of beef
1½ tablespoons olive oil
pinch of salt
pinch of pepper
1 small green pepper, chopped
2 large onions, chopped
2 celery stalks, chopped
6 peppercorns
6 mushrooms, sliced thinly
3 shallots, chopped
⅓ teaspoon tarragon

1) Heat the oil in a pan. Lightly sprinkle the meat with salt and pepper and place in pan. Brown the meat on all sides and remove from pan.

2) Lightly brown the green pepper, onion, and celery in the oil. Lower flame and return the brisket to the pan. Add the peppercorns and cover, simmering for approximately 2½ to 3 hours.

3) Place cooked meat in a pan, and place pan in a preheated oven at 350 degrees. Remove the fat from the gravy and place in a skillet; pour remaining gravy over meat. Add the mushrooms, shallots, and tarragon to the skillet containing the fat and saute until vegetables begin to soften. Spread them over the meat and cook for 30 minutes.

Serves 6

Poor Man's Porterhouse

4 porterhouse steaks, 1 inch thick
1 tablespoon oil
2 teaspoons scallions, chopped finely
2 garlic cloves, crushed
pinch of salt
¼ teaspoon pepper

1) Mix the oil, scallions, garlic, salt, and pepper together and rub over both sides of the steaks. Let marinate for 2 hours at room temperature.

2) Place steaks in preheated broiler and cook for 15 minutes on each side for rare.

Serves 4

Tangy Pot Roast

1 3-pound sirloin tip or rump roast
¼ cup red wine vinegar
¼ cup ketchup
2 tablespoons Worcestershire sauce
2 teaspoons garlic salt
½ teaspoon dry mustard
2 tablespoons soy sauce

1) Brown roast on all sides in a skillet with little oil.

2) Combine all ingredients and pour over meat.

3) Cover and cook at 325 to 350 degrees for 2 hours or until done.

Serves 6

Charlotte Stewart
Panama City, FL

Easy Meat Loaf

3 pounds hamburger
1 pound ground pork
½ cup onion, chopped
½ teaspoon pepper
2 carrots, grated
2 potatoes, grated
1 teaspoon fresh parsley, chopped
4 eggs, beaten
1½ cups milk
4 cups bread crumbs

1) Mix all of the ingredients together.

2) Place into a greased casserole dish and bake in a preheated 350 degree oven for 1 hour.

Serves 8

Blade Steak with Red Wine

4½ pounds blade steak
2 garlic cloves, minced
⅓ cup olive oil
2 tablespoons pepper
2 cups red wine

1) Rub each side of the steak with the garlic and oil. Sprinkle with pepper.

2) Place the steak onto a preheated and greased broiler rack and broil each side for 10 to 12 minutes basting with the wine. Pour the pan juices over the steak and serve.

Serves 6

Fancy Filet Mignon

6 medium size fillets
6 tablespoons oil
2 medium green peppers, sliced thinly
2 medium pimientos, sliced thinly
⅛ pound butter
pinch of salt
pinch of pepper
6 tablespoons sherry

1) Heat 4 tablespoons of the oil in a pan and add green peppers and pimientos. Cover and allow to simmer for 15 to 20 minutes. Heat the butter, salt, pepper and the rest of the oil in another pan.

2) When the buttery mixture begins to bubble rapidly, place fillets in pan and cook for 5 minutes on each side. Lower flame and add in the green peppers, pimientos, and sherry. Cover and simmer for an additional 5 minutes per side.

Serves 6

Mock Chow Mein

1 pound hamburger
1 small onion, chopped
1 cup celery, chopped
2 tablespoons soy sauce
½ cup rice
1 can cream of mushroom soup
1 soup can of water
1 4-ounce can mushrooms

1) Brown hamburger in small amount of fat in skillet. Put remaining ingredients into casserole, using soy sauce instead of salt for seasoning.

2) Bake at least 1 hour at 350 degrees. Mix hamburger into baked ingredients, then serve.

Serves 2

Mrs. Doug Wiarda
Rock Rapids, IA

Fillets Garnished with Baby Squash

6 fillets of beef, 1 inch thick
dash of teaspoon salt
2 tablespoons butter, melted
2 dozen baby squash, cooked
½ teaspoon pepper

1) Lightly sprinkle meat with salt. Lightly brush with melted butter.

2) Place the meat on a broiler rack in a pre-heated oven and broil 5 minutes per side, turning once.

3) Garnish with baby squash.

Serves 6

Quick and Easy Spencer Steak

6 Spencer steaks, 1-inch thick

1) Slice edges of fat to prevent curling.

2) Place steaks on a broiler rack in a preheated oven.

3) Broil for 8 to 10 minutes on each side.

Serves 6

Top Sirloin Blue Bayou

6 top sirloin steaks, ½-pound each
1 tablespoon oil
6 potatoes, sliced thinly
water
1 large onion, sliced thinly
2 teaspoons pepper
¾ teaspoon cayenne pepper
1½ teaspoon paprika
2 tablespoons butter

1) Place the steaks and oil in a pan cook for 5 minutes on each side.

2) Add the potatoes and enough water to cover. Simmer for 15 minutes.

3) Add the onions, pepper, cayenne, and paprika and cook until the liquid has evaporated.

Serves 6

American-Style Enchillada Pie

1 package 12 corn tortillas
2 cans enchillada sauce
1 can V-8 juice
1 medium package Velveeta cheese
2 pounds ground round or chuck
1 green pepper, diced
1 large onion, diced
2 cans chili without beans
salt and pepper to taste
parsley flakes

1) Saute onions and green pepper in butter. Add meat and chili and simmer.

2) Line bottom of large baking pan with 1 layer of tortillas and pour half the V-8 juice over them. Add half the meat mixture, sliced cheese and cover with 1 can enchillada sauce.

3) Repeat with another layer of tortillas, meat mixture and cheese. Cover with another can of enchillada sauce. Crumble remaining tortillas and cheese over the top.

4) Sprinkle with parsley. Bake at 350 degrees for 1 hour.

Serves 6

Charlene L. Adair
Deland, FL

Classic Beef Wellington

1 3-pound fillet
oil
salt
pepper
½ pound butter
¾ pound flour
⅓ ounce salt
2 egg yolks
⅔ cup water
4 ounces pate de foie gras (fresh American
duck liver)
4 medium size truffles, diced
1 egg yolk
½ cup milk

1) Lightly spread oil on the fillet, then lightly season with salt and pepper. Place in a baking pan and bake in a preheated oven at 450 degrees for 45 minutes.

2) Mix the butter, flour, salt and sugar together. Mix the egg yolks with the water and slowly add them to the dry mixture until dough is formed. Roll the dough until it is the proper size to encircle the fillet.

3) Remove cooked fillet and cover with the pate de foie gras and diced truffles. Place the beef on top of the dough, rolling the dough around the edges of the fillet so that it is completely surrounded.

4) Blend 1 egg yolk with milk and lightly brush on top of the dough. Place in over for 15 to 20 minutes or until the dough turns a golden brown.

Serves 4

Beef Short Ribs in Sauce Japanese

3 pounds lean short ribs
2 teaspoons ginger
2 tablespoons honey
2 tablespoons soy sauce
1 garlic clove, minced
1 cup pineapple juice

1) Mix the ginger, honey, soy sauce, garlic and ½ cup pineapple juice together.

2) Place the ribs in the mixture and marinate for 20 minutes, turning often.

3) Remove ribs and place in a broiling pan for 30 minutes. Reserve mixture. Baste often with mixture, turning ribs a few times during cooking.

4) Add the remaining ½ cup pineapple juice to the pan drippings and bring to a boil. Use as a sauce for the cooked ribs.

Serves 4

Hash Casserole

4 cups cooked corned beef, diced
2½ cups potatoes, diced
2 cups onions, chopped
1 cup green peppers, chopped
4 tablespoons parsley, minced
1 teaspoon salt
½ teaspoon pepper
⅓ teaspoon thyme
12 ounces canned beef gravy
1½ teaspoons Worcestershire sauce

1) Mix all of the ingredients together.

2) Place into a greased casserole dish. Cover and bake in a 375 degree oven for 1 hour. Remove cover and cook for 15 additional minutes.

Serves 6 to 8

Steak with Red Wine and Tarragon

6 ½-pound steaks
4 tablespoons butter
6 tablespoons fresh tarragon, chopped
1½ cup red wine
3 tablespoons flour

1) Melt 2 tablespoons of butter in a pan. Place steaks in butter and cook for 5 minutes on each side. Remove.

2) Place the tarragon and red wine in the same pan and simmer for 3 minutes.

3) In a different pan, melt the remaining butter. Stir in the flour, and then slowly pour in the wine with tarragon. Stir until rich and creamy, and pour over the steaks.

Serves 6

Chips 'N Chili (Mexican Lasagna)

1 pound ground beef
1 can tomato paste
½ onion
1 clove garlic
1 can kidney beans
1 teaspoon chili powder
taco sauce to taste
½ bag tortilla chips
various spices to taste
salt, pepper (green/red)
1 cup shredded cheese (your choice)

1) Brown ground beef, drain.

2) Add spices, onion, garlic pepper, tomato paste and beans. Simmer over medium heat for 30 minutes.

3) Layer bottom of a baking dish with half the chips, add half the mixture, more chips, then more mixture. Top with cheese.

4) Bake at 350 degrees for 25 to 30 minutes. Serve immediately.

Serves 4

Mr. Darrell Patterson
Springfield, IL

Shepherd's Stew

2 pounds chuck roll, trimmed and cubed
1¼ teaspoon salt
½ teaspoon pepper
¾ teaspoon cinnamon
¼ cup olive oil
8 small white onions
2 cups beef broth
6 ounces canned tomato sauce
3 cups eggplant, diced
2 small green peppers, sliced thinly
⅓ cup rice

1) Season the meat with 1 teaspoon of salt, pepper, and cinnamon.

2) In a pan, brown the meat in ⅛ cup of oil. Remove. Saute the onions in the same pan until transparent, place meat back in pan.

3) In the oil remaining in the Dutch oven or casserole, saute the onions until golden. Return the meat and add ⅓ cup of the broth and the tomato sauce. Cover and simmer over low flame for 1 hour.

4) Saute the eggplant in the remaining oil for 10 minutes. Sprinkle with remaining salt. Add green peppers, rice, and remaining broth to the meat. Cover and cook for ½ hour.

Serves 4

Western-Style Steak

6 T-bone steaks, ½ to ¾-inch thick
3 tablespoons butter
3 medium onions, sliced thinly
pinch of salt
pinch of pepper

1) Heat butter in a pan until it beigns to sizzle. Add the onions and saute until they turn a golden color.

2) Add the T-bone steaks and saute quickly for 8 minutes, turning once.

Serves 6

Flank Steak—Mushroom Sauce

3 pounds flank steak, cut in cubes
1 cup sliced green onions, tops included
2 packages dry mushroom soup (or 2 cans
condensed soup)
1 cup Burgundy wine
1 cup water
1 tablespoon salt
dash pepper

1) Put Wesson Oil in large skillet and heat. Brown
flank steak, then add water and cook until tender.

2) Mix wine and soup. When meat is almost done,
add salt and pepper and drained mushrooms.

3) Cook 3 more minutes. Add cut up potatoes or
cooked noodles.

Serves 6

Paul W. Wilson
Black Mountain, NC

Filet Mignon A La Cindy

6 thick fillets
Two dozen peppercorns
2 tablespoons butter
1 large garlic clove, minced
6 tablespoons brandy

1) With a fork, pierce both sides of the fillets and place peppercorns inside.

2) Heat 1 tablespoon of butter in a pan until bubbling. Add the garlic and saute until transparent.

3) Cook the fillets in butter and garlic for 8 to 10 minutes on each side. Melt remaining tablespoon of butter in pan, then add the brandy and set on fire. Cook until flame has completely died down. Pour pan juice over fillets and serve.

Serves 6

Pot Roast Italian Style

2 pounds pot roast, trimmed
½ tablespoon olive oil
1 tablespoon butter
1½ garlic cloves, minced
⅓ cup chopped onions
dash of salt
½ teaspoon pepper
½ teaspoon rosemary
2 tablespoons minced parsley
⅓ cup beef broth
1½ tablespoons dry vermouth
6 ounces canned tomato sauce

1) Heat the oil and butter in a pan. Place roast, garlic and onions in the oil and butter and cook until brown on all sides, approximately 10 minutes.

2) Season with the salt, pepper, and rosemary, and then add the parsley, beef broth, vermouth and tomato sauce.

3) Cover and bake in a 350 degree oven for 2½ to 3 hours or until meat is tender.

Serves 4

Ribs and Barbecue Sauce

3 pounds beef ribs
1 jar chili sauce
1 tablespoon Worcestershire sauce
¼ teaspoon cayenne (red) pepper
¾ cup brown sugar
1 bottle ketchup
½ teaspoon dry mustard
1 tablespoon lemon juice
1 small onion, finely chopped

1) Salt and pepper ribs. Bake about 30 to 45 minutes. Add sauce after grease is drained off.

2) Bake another 45 minutes or until done. Smother with sauce and serve.

Serves 4

Pius Kraft
Mandan, ND

Tangy Top Sirloin

2½ pounds top sirloin, 1 inch thick
dash of salt
3 tablespoons salad oil
4 medium onions, sliced thinly
6 green peppers, seeded and cut into strips
1 large garlic clove, minced

1) Saute the green peppers, onions, and garlic in 2 tablespoons of hot oil until slightly tender. Remove and place on a plate.

2) Lightly sprinkle the top sirloin with salt. Saute the steak in the remaining hot oil and cook until tender.

3) Garnish with green peppers, onions and garlic.

Serves 6

Pot Roast A La Hungary

2 pound pot roast, trimmed
dash of salt
½ teaspoon pepper
½ cup flour
1 tablespoon oil
1 cup onions, sliced
4 ounces canned tomato sauce
½ tablespoon paprika
1 teaspoon caraway seeds
¼ cup water

1) Mix the salt, pepper, and flour together and rub it over the pot roast.

2) Heat the oil in a pan. Place meat in oil and cook until brown on all sides, approximately 10 minutes. Place onions in pan and saute until transparent.

3) Add the tomato sauce, paprika, caraway seeds, and water. Cover and simmer over low flame for 2½ to 3 hours or until tender.

Serves 4

Hot Texas Chili

¾ pound boneless beef, trimmed and diced
1 tablespoon oil
1 cup onions, sliced thinly
½ cup green peppers, chopped
1 teaspoon salt
½ teaspoon pepper
½ garlic clove, minced
1 tablespoon chili powder
15 ounces canned tomatoes
8 ounces canned kidney beans

1) Heat the oil in a pan and saute the onions and green peppers for 10 minutes. Add the beef and cook over a medium flame, approximately 10 minutes, until brown.

2) Mix in the salt, pepper, garlic, chili powder, and tomatoes. Cover and cook over a low flame for 2 hours. Add the kidney beans and cook another 15 minutes.

Serves 4

LAMB

Old-Fashioned Irish Stew

1 pound leg of lamb, trimmed and cubed
¼ teaspoon salt
¼ teaspoon pepper
1 bay leaf
1½ cups beef broth
½ pound white turnips, pared and sliced
½ pound carrots, pared and sliced
1 onion, sliced
1½ tablespoons flour
3 tablespoons water

1) Place the lamb, salt, pepper, bay leaf, and broth in a pot and heat to boiling. Lower flame, cover, and simmer for 40 minutes or until meat is almost tender. Remove from heat and refrigerate for 6 hours.

2) Remove the bay leaf and skim off the fat. Heat to boiling, add vegetables, cover and simmer for 30 minutes, or until the vegetables are tender.

3) Mix the flour and water together until smooth. Place into the stew and cook for 3 to 5 minutes, or until the sauce begins to bubble, stirring often.

Serves 4

Greek Lamb

2 pounds leg of lamb, cubed
8 green tomatoes
8 mushroom caps
2 tablespoons olive oil
2 tablespoons molasses
¼ cup raspberry vinegar
¼ cup fresh mint leaves, chopped
dash of salt
¼ teaspoon pepper

1) Mix all of the ingredients together and refrigerate for 2 to 3 hours. Stir once or twice while setting.

2) Place the lamb, tomatoes, and mushrooms on 4 skewers, reserving the marinade. Place the skewers on a grill and cook for 10 to 12 minutes, turning and basting often.

Serves 4

Lamb and Spinach Soup

1½ pounds ground lamb
12 ounces frozen spinach
2 small onions, sliced thinly
4 cups water
⅓ cup precooked rice
1 teaspoon salt
½ teaspoon pepper
⅓ teaspoon paprika
⅓ cup parsley, chopped
1½ cups sour cream
2 egg yolks, beaten

1) Saute the lamb in a pot over a low flame until the lamb begins to brown. Drain off the fat.

2) Add the spinach and onions and cook uncovered for 5 to 7 minutes, or until the spinach has thawed. Add the water, rice, salt, pepper, paprika, and parsley, and bring to a boil. Lower heat, and simmer for 12 to 15 minutes.

3) Blend the sour cream and egg yolks until rich and creamy. Spoon four tablespoons of the soup into the creamy mixture, stir until blended, and then add the mixture to the soup.

Serves 6

Traditional Leg of Lamb

3 pound leg of lamb
½ teaspoon salt
½ teaspoon pepper
1 large garlic clove, minced
½ teaspoon rosemary
¼ cup butter, melted

1) Mix the garlic, rosemary, salt and pepper together and rub into the lamb. Let sit for 1 hour.

2) Place the seasoned lamb on a rack in a roasting pan and roast in a 375 degree oven for 45 minutes to 1 hour or until meat is tender. Baste often with the melted butter.

Serves 4

Rack of Lamb A La Orange

4 pound rack of lamb
1 teaspoon salt
½ cup orange marmalade
½ cup lemon juice

1) Rub the lamb with salt and cover the tip of each bone with aluminum foil. Place on a rack in a shallow roasting pan and roast at 375 degrees for 45 minutes.

2) Mix the orange marmalade and lemon juice. Brush one-half of the sauce on the lamb.

3) Continue to roast the lamb, uncovered, for an additional 45 minutes. Brush with the remaining sauce and roast for an additional 30 minutes.

Serves 4

Curried Leg of Lamb

4 pound leg of lamb
1 small garlic clove, minced
¾ tablespoon fresh rosemary leaves
⅓ teaspoon celery salt
⅓ teaspoon onion powder
⅓ teaspoon pepper
¾ tablespoon curry powder
¾ cup water
¾ cup red wine
4 carrots
4 stalks celery
8 small potatoes
8 small white onions

1) Slice pockets in the lamb and place rosemary and garlic inside. Season with the celery salt, onion powder, and pepper. Rub the curry powder on the lamb.

2) Place the lamb on a rack in a roasting pan. Add the wine and water to the pan, and arrange the vegetables around the lamb. Place in a preheated oven at 500 degrees and cook for 12 minutes. Lower the heat to 350 degrees and cook for 1 hour, basting twice during cooking.

Serves 4

Classic Baked Lamb

2 pounds breast of lamb, cubed
salt
pepper
¾ cup red wine
⅓ cup water
⅓ cup red currant jelly
1½ tablespoons parsley, chopped
1½ teaspoons marjoram

1) Lightly season the lamb with salt and pepper and place in a roasting pan. Bake in a preheated oven at 375 degrees for 1 hour, or until slightly tender.

2) Combine the remaining ingredients and bring to a boil. Pour the mixture over the lamb and bake for 25 minutes or until lamb is glazed and tender, basting often.

Serves 4

Special Baked Lamb

1 pound lean lamb shoulder, cubed and browned
dash of pepper
⅓ teaspoon crushed cumin seeds
⅓ teaspoon crushed coriander seeds
¾ cup onion, chopped
1½ cups water
½ cup wheat pilaf
¾ cup celery, diced
½ teaspoon salt

1) Place lamb, pepper, coriander and cumin seeds in a baking dish.

2) Saute the onions until transparent, add water, wheat pilaf, celery, and salt, and heat to boiling. Pour hot mixture over the lamb and mix lightly. Cover and bake at 350 degrees for 1 hour, or until lamb is tender.

Serves 4

Lamb in Dijon and Red Currant Sauce

6 lamb chops
2 teaspoons Dijon mustard
¾ cup red currant jelly
1 large lemon
3 teaspoons lemon peel, grated
½ teaspoon salt

1) Heat all of the ingredients with the exception of the lamb over a low flame until the red currant jelly melts. Remove from heat.

2) Place the lamb chops on a rack in a broiling pan and broil for 7 minutes. Turn the chops over, brush with the sauce and broil for 7 minutes longer, brushing often.

Serves 6

Lamb with Rice

1½ pounds ground lamb
3 tablespoons butter, melted
2 small onions, diced
3 cups precooked rice
3 tablespoons black currants, dried
⅓ teaspoon allspice
1½ tablespoon parsley, dehydrated
6 bouillon cubes
3 cups warm water
1½ cup canned tomatoes
1 teaspoon salt
½ teaspoon pepper

1) Cook the lamb in melted butter in a pot until lamb is browned. Add the onion, and cook until it becomes transparent. Add the rice, black currants, allspice, and parsley. Cook for 8 to 10 minutes, stirring constantly.

2) Dissolve the bouillon in the water and pour over the lamb. Add the tomatoes, salt, and pepper, stirring well.

3) Simmer over a low flame for 25 minutes.

Serves 6

Hot and Spicy Roast Leg of Lamb

3 pound leg of lamb
⅓ cup chili sauce
¾ cup red wine
1½ tablespoons vinegar
⅓ cup beef broth
1 tablespoon oil
1 teaspoon salt
½ teaspoon pepper
½ tablespoon sugar
1 bay leaf, crushed
¾ cup onions, minced
1 small garlic clove, minced

1) Mix all of the ingredients and pour over the leg of lamb. Let marinate in the refrigerator for at least 12 hours, turning a number of times.

2) Place the lamb on a rack in a roasting pan, add half of the marinade and cook in a 325 degree oven for 2½ to 3 hours or until the lamb is tender. Baste often with the remaining marinade.

Serves 4

Lamb Medallions Hollandaise

8 lamb medallions
⅓ cup hazelnuts, toasted, skinned and crushed
¾ tablespoon unsalted butter, room temperature
1 tablespoon lemon juice
2 egg yolks
¾ cup plus 2 tablespoons butter
dash of cayenne pepper

1) Mix the hazelnuts and ½ tablespoon of butter together. Blend the lemon juice, egg yolks, ¾ cup butter, and cayenne pepper together until smooth and rich. Add the hazelnuts and mix well and keep warm.

2) Lightly season the lamb with salt and pepper, and saute in the remaining butter for 5 minutes on each side. Spoon the warm hollandaise sauce on top of the medallions and serve.

Serves 4

Easy Broiled Lamb

6 lamb steaks (1 inch thick)
1 tablespoon oil
oregano
salt
pepper

1) Mix the oil, oregano, salt, and pepper together. Rub on the lamb steaks. Let marinate for 30 minutes.

2) Place lamb in a preheated broiler and broil for 5 minutes on each side.

Serves 6

Broiled Lamb with Marjoram

16 ounce lamb leg steak, trimmed
¼ teaspoon pepper
1 teaspoon garlic salt
2 tablespoons marjoram leaves, crushed

1) Season the lamb with the pepper and garlic salt. Rub with marjoram.

2) Place steak on the rack of broiler pan and broil for 7 to 10 minutes on each side.

Serves 4

Lamb Shish Kebabs

1½ pounds lamb, cubed
¾ cup red wine
2 tablespoons salad oil
¾ teaspoon salt
¾ teaspoon oregano leaves
2 small green peppers, cut into 12 pieces
1 large onion, cut into 12 pieces
6 ounces pimientos, drained and cut into 12 pcs.
¾ pound mushrooms

1) Mix the lamb, wine, oil, oregano, and salt together.

2) Place the lamb and vegetables on skewers and brush with the marinade. Broil for 20 to 25 minutes, brushing and turning skewers often.

Serves 6

Seasoned Lamb

3 pounds ground lamb
1½ cup bread crumbs
3 tablespoons celery, chopped
3 tablespoons onion, chopped
3 tablespoons fresh dill weed
1½ teaspoons salt
½ teaspoon pepper
3 eggs

1) Mix all of the ingredients together and place into a well-oiled loaf pan.

2) Bake at 375 degrees for 1 hour.

Serves 6

Baked Lamb and Artichoke Hearts

2 pounds shoulder of lamb, cubed
1 tablespoon butter, melted
1 teaspoon salt
½ teaspoon pepper
⅓ cup dry vermouth
10 ounces frozen artichoke hearts, cooked
and drained
3 eggs
⅓ cup Parmesan cheese, grated
1½ tablespoons parsley, minced

1) Cook the lamb in melted butter in a pan until lamb is browned. Season with the salt and pepper, and add the vermouth. Cook over a high flame for 5 minutes.

2) Cover and bake in a 350 degree oven for 30 minutes. Add the artichoke hearts, cover, and bake for an additional 10 to 12 minutes.

3) Blend the eggs, cheese and parsley together, pour over the lamb and artichokes, and bake uncovered for an additional 10 to 12 minutes.

Serves 4

Lamb and Fruit Stew

3 pounds lamb shoulder, cubed
⅓ cup flour
salt
pepper
2 tablespoons oil
¾ cup bouillon
¾ cup celery, chopped
2 small onions, chopped
1 small green pepper, chopped
1 orange, peeled and sliced
1 apple, peeled, cored, and sliced
⅓ cup apricot brandy

1) Mix the flour, salt, and pepper together. Dip lamb into mixture. Place coated lamb into hot oil and brown. Add the bouillon and bring to a boil. Lower the flame and add the fruits and vegetables.

2) Cover and simmer covered for 1 hour, stirring occasionally. Add the brandy and simmer for an additional 30 minutes.

Serves 4

Lamb Chops with Mushrooms

6 lamb chops
4 tablespoons butter, melted
¾ pound mushrooms, diced
3 tablespoons green onions, minced
¼ teaspoon salt
¼ teaspoon savory
⅓ cup water
2 cups bread cubes

1) Saute the mushrooms, onions, salt, and savory in the melted butter until the vegetables are soft. Remove from flame and add the water and bread cubes. Mix well.

2) Slice each lamb chop to form a pocket, and place the mixture into the pocket; close with toothpicks.

3) Place the lamb chops on a rack iin a broiling pan and broil for 15 minutes, turning once.

Serves 6

Sauteed Lamb Cakes

4 cups cooked lamb, chopped
1 cup onions, chopped
2 tablespoons butter, melted
6 cooked potatoes, peeled and chopped
2 tablespoons catsup
2 eggs

1) Saute the onions in the melted butter until transparent. Add the lamb, potatoes, catsup, and egg. Mix well.

2) Form 16 patties, and saute for 5 minutes on each side, or until thoroughly browned.

Serves 8

PORK AND HAM

Baby Meat Loaf

½ **pound ground ham**
½ **pound ground beef**
⅓ **cup instant mashed potatoes**
⅓ **cup condensed milk**
2 **eggs, beaten**
¾ **cup bread crumbs**
½ **teaspoon salt**
½ **teaspoon pepper**
¾ **cup water**
2 **bouillon cubes**

1) Mix the ham, beef and potatoes together. Stir in the milk and eggs. Add the bread crumbs, salt and pepper. Form into four small loaves. Place in a well-oiled baking dish.

2) Dissolve bouillon cubes in water. Pour liquid into baking dish. Cover the dish with foil.

3) Place dish in a 375 degree oven for 50 minutes to 1 hour. Remove foil and place under a broiler for 3 to 5 minutes, until tops are browned.

Serves 4

Chinese Pork Chops

8 pork chops, ¼-inch thick
1 tablespoon oil
1 small garlic clove, crushed
1 teaspoon ground ginger
3 tablespoons sake
⅓ cup soy sauce

1) Mix oil, garlic, ginger, sake, and soy sauce together in a marinating dish. Place pork chops in sauce and marinate in the refrigerator for 6 hours, turning once.

2) Remove marinated pork chops and cook in well-oiled pan for five minutes on each side, or until meat is tender.

Serves 4

Baked Ham with Dijon Mustard

2 pounds ham, sliced 1-inch thick
Dijon mustard
⅓ cup brown sugar
¾ cup pineapple syrup
8 pineapple slices

1) Place the ham into a baking dish and spread with dijon and brown sugar. Pour on the pineapple syrup.

2) Place into a preheated oven at 350 degrees and bake for 1 to 1¼ hours, basting often.

3) Set the slices of pineapple on top of the ham and cook for an additional 15 minutes until the pineapple is browned.

Serves 6

Pork Pot Pie

1 pound pork chops
2 green peppers
4 medium white potatoes
1 small onion (optional)
salt to taste

Dumplings:
2 cups flour
⅓ cup shortening
½ teaspoon salt
¼ cup water (plus 2 tablespoons, if needed)

1) Cut meat in 1½ inch pieces. Cut 1 green pepper into ½ inch squares. Mix with chopped onion and salt, place in dutch oven with 1 quart water.

2) Bring to a boil on top of the stove, then cook covered over medium heat for 1 hour. Add potatoes cut into 1½ inch pieces.

3) Meanwhile, for dumplings, mix flour, shortening, salt and water. Mix well and cut into 2-inch squares. Add with chopped green pepper. Cook covered 20 minutes.

Serves 4

Mrs. Harry A. Russel
Venice, FL

Classic Meat Loaf

⅓ **pound ground ham**
⅓ **pound ground pork**
⅓ **pound ground veal**
2 eggs
¼ **teaspoon salt**
¼ **teaspoon pepper**
2 tablespoons packaged onion soup
6 ounces cream of mushroom soup
3 tablespoons flour
⅓ **cup bread crumbs**

1) Mix the ham, pork, and veal together. Add the eggs, salt, and pepper. Mix well. Stir in the onion soup, mushroom soup and flour.

2) Coat a well-oiled casserole dish with the bread crumbs. Pour in the meat mixture, spreading evenly.

3) Place the casserole in a 375 degree oven and bake for 1 hour.

Serves 4

Pork and Pear Stew

6 pound pork shoulder, boned and cubed
1 tablespoon oil
2 medium onions, sliced thinly
2 teaspoons salt
1 teaspoon pepper
3 large pears, pared and sliced
6 celery ribs, sliced
6 carrots, sliced

1) Saute the onions in the oil until onions are transparent.

2) Lightly season the pork with the salt and pepper, add to onions and brown. Add the remaining ingredients, cover, and bring to boil. Lower flame and simmer for 1½ to 2 hours or until the pork is tender.

Serves 6

Barbecued Baked Pork Ribs (Chinese)

3 pounds pork ribs, washed and cut into slices
2 tablespoons Hoi-sin sauce
3 tablespoons molasses
3 tablespoons Sweet & Sour sauce
3 tablespoons vinegar
3 tablespoons Kraft barbecue sauce
1 clove minced garlic

1) Combine all ingredients. Pour over ribs. Cover with foil. Bake at 350 degrees for 2 hours.

2) Remove ribs, put on cookie sheet. Place in oven and broil on both sides. Use the juice left in the pan to make gravy, and pour over cooked noodles.

Serves 6

Mrs. Robert J. Carlson
Puta Gorda, FL

Mexican Stew

2 pounds pork, trimmed and cubed
3 onions, sliced
2 tablespoons oil
3 cups canned tomatoes
⅓ cup green pepper, chopped
⅓ cup celery, chopped
1½ tablespoons chili powder
1 teaspoon salt
1½ tablespoons flour
3 tablespoons water

1) Brown the pork and onions in oil.

2) Add the remaining ingredients, cover, and simmer over a low flame for 1 to 1¼ hours.

Serves 6

Hamburgers with Sweet Potatoes

½ pound lean ground pork
½ pound ground beef
¼ teaspoon salt
¼ teaspoon pepper
1 tablespoon butter
12 ounces canned sweet potatoes, drained
⅓ cup dried currants
⅓ cup raisins
4 pineapple rings

1) Mix the pork, beef, salt, and pepper together. Form into four equal patties. Brown the patties in melted butter.

2) Mash the sweet potatoes until soft and light. Stir in the dried currants and raisins.

3) Place the sweet potato mixture in a well-oiled casserole dish. Set the pineapple rings on top, pressing them into the mixture. Place one hamburger patty on top of each pineapple ring.

4) Bake in a preheated 350 degree oven for 30 to 35 minutes.

Serves 4

Pork Vermouth

5 pounds boneless pork roast
⅔ cup dry vermouth
½ teaspoon nutmeg
2 teaspoons seasoned salt
2 teaspoons dried sage
½ teaspoon pepper

Sauce:
1 tablespoon olive oil
2 green onions, chopped
½ teaspoon, thyme
1 tablespoon chopped parsley
¼ teaspoon hickory salt
½ cup condensed chicken broth
⅔ cup dry vermouth
cornstarch for thickening

1) Roast pork according to weight. Use basting sauce frequently during roasting.

2) After roasting and when ready to serve mix the sauce ingredients together and heat on stove.

Serves 6

Marcia S. Galliday
White Port, VA

Pork Midwestern Style

1½ pound pork tenderloin
4 tablespoons water
2 eggs, beaten
½ teaspoon rosemary, crushed
½ teaspoon salt
1½ cup bread crumbs
4 tablespoons oil

1) Split the pork open lengthwise in half, without cutting all the way through. Open meat up and spread flat. Pound the pork to ¼ inch thickness and cut into 6 serving sized pieces.

2) Blend water, eggs, rosemary, and salt together. Spread bread crumbs on wax paper.

3) Dip the pork into the mixture, then dip in the bread crumbs.

4) Fry coated pork in oil for 10 to 12 minutes or until meat is tender, turning once.

Serves 6

Fried Ham and Cheese Sandwich

6 ham slices
6 Swiss cheese slices
3 eggs, beaten
1½ cups milk
¼ teaspoon pepper
3 tablespoons butter
12 bread slices

1) Lightly butter the slices of bread. Place a slice of ham and cheese on 6 of the buttered slices. Tightly place other 6 slices on top of ham and cheese.

2) Mix the eggs, milk and pepper together. Dip the sandwiches in the mixture.

3) Fry the coated sandwiches in butter until the cheese is melted and bread is browned.

Serves 6

Sherry Hamburgers

¾ pound lean ground pork
¾ pound ground beef
2 tablespoons butter, melted
2 eggs, beaten
¼ teaspoon salt
¼ teaspoon pepper
Juice of 1 lemon
¾ tablespoon lemon rind, grated
2 tablespoons parsley, dried
¾ cup bread crumbs
2 tablespoons onion, dried
⅓ cup sherry
6 hamburger buns

1) Mix the ground pork and ground beef together. Stir in 1 tablespoon melted butter, eggs, salt, and pepper. Add the lemon juice, lemon rind, parsley, bread crumbs and onion. Mix well. Form mixture into 6 patties.

2) Brown the patties in the remaining butter. Add the wine, lower the flame, and simmer 25 to 30 minutes, turning the patties often.

Serves 6

Curry Pork Chops

pork chops (1 per serving)
½ teaspoon salt
2 cans cream of chicken soup
cooked rice
¾ cup flour
½ teaspoon curry powder
1½ cups milk

1) Mix flour, salt, and curry powder in paper bag. Shake pork chops one at a time in bag.

2) Brown quickly on both sides in frying pan with a little melted shortening. Mix soup and milk, pour over pork chops. Sprinkle with curry powder. Simmer until tender.

3) Serve over hot rice. Garnish with green pepper ring.

Lillian Fry
Provo, UT

Tangy Pork Chops

6 pork chops, 1 inch thick
4 tablespoons flour
3 teaspoons dry mustard
3 tablespoons paprika
1 teaspoon salt
3 tablespoons olive oil
2 onions, minced
3 cups canned tomatoes
3 tablespoons Worcestershire sauce
3 tablespoons catsup

1) Mix the flour, mustard, paprika, and salt together. Coat the pork chops with the mixture and fry in the olive oil until browned. Sprinkle with onions.

2) Mix the tomatoes, Worcestershire sauce, and catsup. Spoon over the browned pork chops.

3) Cover and cook over a low flame for 30 minutes.

Serves 6

Quick and Easy Ham Casserole

3 cups ham, cubed and cooked
2 tablespoons butter
⅓ cup cream
⅓ teaspoon basil
dash of salt
dash of pepper
1½ pounds canned macaroni
½ cup cheese, grated
1½ cup bread crumbs

1) Quickly saute the cooked ham in butter, cream, basil, salt and pepper.

2) Place the macaroni in a well-oiled casserole dish. Set ham on top. Sprinkle with cheese and crumbs.

3) Place casserole in a 350 degree oven for 30 minutes.

Serves 6

Baked English Burgers

¾ pound ground pork
¾ pound ground beef
½ teaspoon nutmeg
½ teaspoon pepper
½ teaspoon salt
1 tablespoon oil

Batter:
1 cup flour
¾ cup milk
1 egg
¼ teaspoon salt

1) Mix the ground pork, ground beef, nutmeg, salt, and pepper. Form into 12 small patties. Brown patties in oil.

2) Blend the flour, milk, egg, and salt together. Set aside until the browned patties have cooled. Pour the batter over the cooled patties, place in 350 degree oven, and bake for 25 to 30 minutes.

Serves 6

Traditional Ham and Beans

1½ pounds ham
water
1½ cups beans
2 small onions, sliced
⅓ cup black molasses
2 teaspoons dry mustard

1) Place the ham in a pot, cover with water and bring to a boil. Lower flame and simmer for 3 hours or until the meat is tender.

2) Remove ham, dice, and return to broth. Add the remaining ingredients, cover, and simmer for an additional 3 hours.

Serves 4

Sauerkraut and Fresh Kielbasa

1 large can sauerkraut, drained
1½ pound fresh Kielbasa, cut into 3 to 4 slices
2 medium onions, diced
¼ teaspoon pepper
½ pound bacon
½ teaspoon caraway seeds
2 cans water (make sure there is water in pot while cooking)

1) In large fry pan, fry bacon, remove and add onions to bacon fat. Fry until light in color. Drain and cut into small pieces.

2) In large pot put sauerkraut, caraway seeds and pepper. Add onions, bacon grease and bacon. Fry fresh kielbasa until brown. Add to sauerkraut. Add water, cover and cook for about 2½ hours. Serve with mashed potatoes.

Serves 4

Mrs. Elsie Sierleja
Rock Creek, OH

Hot and Spicy Casserole

½ pound lean ground pork
½ pound ground beef
1½ cups noodles, cooked
6 ounces canned tomato sauce
1 small green pepper, diced
1½ cups onion, diced
2 pimentos, sliced
1½ cups American cheese, diced
⅓ teaspoon paprika
⅓ cup parsley, minced
½ teaspoon salt
½ teaspoon pepper
3 strips bacon, diced

1) Mix together all of the ingredients with the exception of the bacon. Sprinkle the bacon on the botoom of a well-oiled casserole dish. Place the mixture on top of the bacon, spreading evenly.

2) Bake in a 350 degree oven for 50 minutes to 1 hour.

Serves 6

VARIETY MEATS

Chicken Livers
with Chopped Shallots

2 pounds chicken livers
2 tablespoons butter
¼ teaspoon rosemary
dash of salt
dash of pepper
16 shallots, chopped
1 cup white wine

1) Place chicken livers in butter and brown for 5 minutes per side. Lightly season with rosemary, salt, and pepper.

2) Stir in the chopped shallots and white wine. Lower flame and simmer for 10 to 12 minutes.

Serves 4

New Orleans Style Tongue

2 pounds beef tongue
1 teaspoon salt
1 small onion, sliced
¼ cup white raisins
½ garlic clove
1 bay leaf
⅓ cup ketchup

1) Lightly season the beef tongue with salt. Place seasoned tongue in a roasting pan in an oven at 325 degrees and cook for 45 minutes to 1 hour, or until skin can be removed.

2) Remove skin, return to roasting pan, add remaining ingredients, and cook until tender.

Serves 4

Sweetbreads in a Sherry and Cream Sauce

2 pairs calf's sweetbreads, parboiled and sliced diagonally
¼ cup flour
2 tablespoons butter, melted
1½ tablespoons warm cognac
2 small truffles, sliced
⅓ pound mushrooms, sliced
⅛ teaspoon nutmeg
½ teaspoon salt
⅛ teaspoon pepper
⅓ cup sweet sherry
¾ cup heavy cream

1) Coat the sweetbreads in the flour and brown in the butter.

2) Pour the cognac over the browned sweetbreads and set on fire. Add the truffles, mushrooms, nutmeg, salt, and pepper. Cook over a low flame for 5 minutes.

3) Stir in the sherry and cook for an additional 5 minutes. Mix in the cream and simmer for 3 minutes.

Serves 4

Classic Beef Tongue

3 pounds beef tongue
water
1 bay leaf
6 peppercorns
1 tablespoon salt

1) Place the beef tongue into a pot with enough boiling water to cover. Add bay leaf, peppercorns, and salt.

2) Cover and cook over a low flame for 2 to 2½ hours. Remove, peel off the skin, and return the beef tongue to the still boiling water for 5 minutes, or until heated through.

Serves 6

Traditional Liver and Onions

6 calf's liver slices, ¾ inch thick
dash of salt
dash of pepper
¾ cup bread crumbs, toasted
3 large onions, sliced
3 tablespoons shortening, melted

1) Lightly season the liver with salt and pepper, then coat in the bread crumbs.

2) Saute the onions in shortening until brown. Place the seasoned liver in onions and cook for 5 minutes on each side.

Serves 6

Calf's Sweetbreads with Ham

2 pairs calf's sweetbreads, parboiled
⅓ cup flour
2 tablespoons olive oil
⅓ cup ham, cooked
¾ cup mushrooms, sliced
½ cup tomatoes, peeled and diced
⅓ cup white wine
2 tablespoons butter
½ teaspoon salt
¼ teaspoon pepper

1) Lightly coat the calf's sweetbreads in the flour. Brown the coated sweetbreads in the oil.

2) Drain excess oil, add ham, mushrooms, tomatoes, wine, butter, salt, and pepper. Bring to a boil and cook over a low flame for 10 to 12 minutes.

Serves 4

Kidney and Red Wine Stew

3 pounds beef kidneys, trimmed and cubed
2 garlic cloves, split
1 cup chopped onions
bacon fat
flour
½ teaspoon salt
½ teaspoon pepper
1½ cups red wine
1½ cups consomme

1) Saute the garlic and onions in the bacon fat.

2) Coat the kidneys with the flour, place in the skillet, and cook until browned.

3) Lightly season with salt and pepper, add the red wine and consomme, and simmer for 1 to 1½ hours, or until kidneys are tender.

Serves 8

Gourmet Calf's Brains

4 large sets calf's brains
water
pinch of salt
2 tablespoons vinegar
⅓ pound butter, melted
1 pound mushrooms, sliced
2 tablespoons capers
4 tablespoons parsley, chopped
2 teaspoons lemon juice
pinch of pepper

1) Place the calf's brains, salt, and vinegar in boiling water. Boil for 10 minutes, then remove and place in cold water. Let cool, remove skin and veins, drain, and cut in half.

2) Saute the prepared brains in butter, remove and drain on paper towels. Place mushrooms in butter and cook until soft. Add capers, parsley, and lemon juice.

3) Return the drained brains to the pan, lightly season with pepper, simmer until cooked through, stirring often.

Serves 8

Broiled Lamb Kidneys

6 lamb kidneys
dash of salt
dash of pepper
1 tablespoon vegetable oil

1) Lightly season the lamb kidneys with salt and pepper. Brush lightly with oil, place on a rack in the broiler and cook for 6 to 8 minutes on each side.

Serves 6

Oxtails with Pork

3 oxtails, sliced into 1 inch pieces
water
¾ cup flour
4 slices pork, diced
2 small carrots, grated
1½ cup onions, diced
1 teaspoon salt
1 teaspoon pepper
6 cups red wine
3 teaspoons tomato paste
1½ cup water

1) Place the oxtails in enough boiling water to cover and cook for 5 minutes. Drain and dry, then coat with flour. Brown the pork in a casserole dish, then drain off the fat, leaving about 2 tablespoons.

2) Add the coated oxtails, carrots, and onions, and cook until browned. Mix in salt, pepper, and 3 cups of wine.

3) Cook over a high flame until the wine has evaporated. Add the tomato paste, remaining wine, and 1½ cups water. Cover and cook over a low flame for 3 to 3½ hours.

Serves 6

VEAL

Veal Marsala Classico

6 veal cutlets, pounded to ⅛ inch thickness
dash of salt
dash of pepper
⅓ cup flour
3 tablespoons butter
⅔ cup Marsala wine

1) Lightly season veal with salt and pepper, then lightly coat with flour.

2) Cook coated and seasoned veal in melted butter over a medium flame until browned. Remove.

3) Add Marsala wine to the pan drippings and cook for 1 minute, stirring often. Pour over veal and serve.

Serves 6

Veal Loaf

1 pound ground veal
⅓ pound ground pork
⅓ cup sour cream
2 carrots, grated
2 tablespoons onion, grated
1 teaspoon salt
¼ teaspoon pepper
¾ teaspoon fresh sage, chopped
½ teaspoon lemon rind, grated

1) Mix all of the ingredients together and place into a baking loaf pan. Bake at 375 for 1¼ hours.

Serves 4

Classic Veal Scallopini

6 veal scallops (¼ pound each)
2 tablespoons butter
⅔ pound mushrooms, sliced
1 onion, finely chopped
1 garlic clove, crushed
1¾ cups fresh tomatoes, peeled and chopped
½ cup white wine
dash of salt
¼ teaspoon dried tarragon leaves, crushed
⅛ teaspoon Parmesan cheese, grated

1) Saute the mushrooms in ½ tablespoon of butter for 5 minutes. Add the garlic and onion and continue to saute until the onion is transparent.

2) Stir in the tomatoes, salt, tarragon, and wine. Lower heat, cover, and simmer for 30 minutes. Stir a few times while cooking.

3) Lightly season the veal with salt and pepper. Place veal in another pan with remaining butter and saute until lightly browned. Pour sauce from other pan over veal, cover, and simmer for 5 minutes. Remove and sprinkle with Parmesan cheese and serve.

Serves 6

Veal with Mushroom and Sour Cream Gravy

1 pound veal steaks, cubed
1 tablespoon oil
8 ounces canned mushroom gravy
⅓ cup water
6 ounces sour cream
⅓ cup parsley, chopped

1) Saute the veal in the oil over a medium flame for 5 minutes on each side. Remove and keep warm.

2) Remove fat from the pan. Add water and mushroom gravy. Heat over high flame until boiling, stirring continuously. Lower flame and simmer for a few minutes.

3) Place sour cream in a bowl. Add ¾ cup of the hot gravy and the parsley to the sour cream, return to the pan and cook for one minute on medium flame. Spoon over veal and serve.

Serves 4

Veal Stuffed with Rice

6 pound breast of veal
oil
1½ cups rice, cooked
1 large garlic clove, minced
1 large onion, chopped
½ teaspoon pepper
¾ teaspoon rosemary
½ teaspoon thyme

1) Cut a pocket into the breast of veal.

2) Mix the cooked rice, garlic, onion, and seasonings together, and stuff the mixture into the pocket of the breast. Use toothpicks to fasten.

3) Place the breast into a baking dish, lightly brush with oil, cover, and bake at 350 degrees for 3 hours.

4) Remove cover and continue cooking for ½ hour longer or until meat is tender. Cut open between the ribs and serve.

Serves 6

Veal Chops with Tarragon

6 veal cutlets, ½ inch thick
pinch of salt
pinch of pepper
⅓ cup flour
2 tablespoons olive oil
1½ cups white wine
¾ teaspoon tarragon
⅓ cup parsley, chopped

1) Lightly season the veal with salt and pepper. Lighty dust seasoned veal with flour.

2) Saute the cutlets in the olive oil until browned. Add the wine, tarragon, and parsley, cover, and cook for 20 to 25 minutes.

Serves 6

Veal in a Creamy Brown Sauce

1½ pound veal scallopini, sliced thinly
3 tablespoons butter
1 tablespoon chopped shallots
⅓ cup heavy cream
¼ teaspoon nutmeg, grated
dash of salt
dash of pepper
¼ cup canned brown sauce
2 tablespoons parsley, chopped

1) Cook the veal in melted butter until veal turns white. Remove and keep warm. Place the shallots in the pan and cook for 1 minute. Add the wine and cook until almost all of it has evaporated.

2) Return the veal to the pan, and add the cream, nutmeg, salt, and pepper. Bring the mixture to a boil, lower flame, and simmer for a few minutes. Stir in the brown sauce and bring to a boil. Sprinkle parsley on top and serve.

Serves 4

Veal Italiano

6 veal cutlets, pounded to ⅛ inch thickness
4 tablespoons butter or margarine (½ stick)
⅓ cup medium sherry
⅓ pound prosciutto, sliced thinly
⅓ pound provolone cheese, grated

1) Lightly brown the veal in melted butter over a medium flame. Place browned veal in a baking dish.

2) Add the sherry to the pan drippings, stir, and pour over the veal. Place prosciutto over the veal. Bake in a preheated oven for 5 to 7 minutes at 350 degrees.

3) Remove from oven and sprinkle the provolone over the veal. Bake 5 to 7 minutes longer, or until the cheese has melted.

Serves 6

Leg of Veal

2 pound leg of veal, boned and tied
½ garlic clove, minced
1 teaspoon salt
½ teaspoon pepper
2 carrots, diced
2 onions, quartered
1 fresh bay leaf
⅛ teaspoon thyme
½ cup white wine
¼ cup butter, melted

1) Mix together the garlic, salt, and pepper and rub into the veal.

2) Place the seasoned veal in a roasting pan and roast in a 375 degree oven for 20 to 25 minutes.

3) Drain the fat. Add the carrots, onions, bay leaf, wine, and melted butter. Reduce the oven temperature to 300 degrees and continue to roast for another 1½ to 2 hours longer, or until meat is tender. Baste often.

Serves 4

Veal A L'Anna

3 pounds veal shoulder, cubed
2 tablespoons cooking oil
¾ cup green pepper, chopped
3 onions, chopped
¾ garlic clove, crushed
2 tablespoons paprika
1½ cups canned tomatoes
1 teaspoon salt
1½ cups water

1) Place the veal, green pepper, onions, and garlic in hot oil and cook for 10 to 12 minutes, stirring continuously.

2) Mix in the paprika, tomatoes, salt, and water. Cover and continue cooking 1 to ½ hours or until meat is tender.

Serves 6

Classic Wiener Schnitzel

1 pound veal steak
⅓ cup bread crumbs
1 tablespoon butter
¾ teaspoon instant beef broth
⅓ cup water, boiling
2 tablespoons lemon juice
dash of salt
⅛ teaspoon pepper
2 tablespoons parsley, chopped

1) Coat each side of the veal steak in the bread crumbs.

2) Brown coated veal in hot butter over medium flame. Place beef broth in boiling water, stir and place into pan with veal. Add lemon juice, salt, pepper, and parsley. Cover and cook over medium flame until boiling. Lower flame and simmer for 30 minutes.

3) Remove steak, spoon pan juices over it, and serve.

Serves 4

Italian Veal Stew

6 veal shank crosscuts
dash of salt
dash of pepper
⅓ cup flour
2 tablespoons olive oil
2 medium onions, chopped
4 tomatoes, peeled and chopped
3 garlic cloves, pressed
¼ teaspoon thyme
1 large leek
1½ cup white wine
1½ cup water
juice of 2 lemons

1) Lightly season the veal with the salt and pepper. Lightly dust the seasoned veal with flour.

2) Brown the veal in hot oil. Remove.

3) Add the remaining ingredients to the pan, with the exception of the lemon juice. Cook for 10 minutes. Place the browned veal into the pan, cover, and cook over a low flame for 1½ to 2 hours or until veal is tender. Add the lemon juice and serve.

Serves 6

Veal with Artichoke Hearts

4 pounds veal cutlet, pounded thin and cut in 16 pieces
4 tablespoons butter
8 frozen artichoke hearts, thawed and drained
2 teaspoons salt
2 eggs, beaten
½ teaspoon pepper
½ cup flour
4 tablespoons oil
½ cup beef broth
⅔ cup Parmesan cheese, grated

1) Saute the thawed artichoke hearts in melted butter for 5 minutes. Remove.

2) Coat the veal with the egg. Mix the salt, pepper, and flour together. Dip the egg-coated veal in the mixture.

3) Brown the coated veal in hot oil. Place the artichokes over the veal, pour on the beef broth, and sprinkle the Parmesan over the top. Place in oven at 375 degrees for 10 to 15 minutes or until top is browned.

Serves 8

Special Veal Chops

4 veal chops
½ teaspoon salt
¼ teaspoon pepper
¼ cup oil
⅓ cup onions, chopped
¼ cup chicken broth
½ cup carrots, sliced
6 ounces canned tomatoes
2 tablespoons parsley, chopped
4 ounces mushrooms, drained and sliced

1) Lightly season veal chops with salt and pepper. Place seasoned chops and onion in hot oil and cook until browned.

2) Add the chicken broth, carrots, and tomatoes. Lower flame, cover, and simmer for 45 minutes to 1 hour or until veal is tender.

3) Add the parsley and mushrooms. Cook uncovered for 5 minutes. Remove veal chops, spoon sauce over them and serve.

Serves 4

Sauteed Veal with Potatoes

2 pounds breast of veal, cut into 2 inch pieces
dash of salt
1½ tablespoons flour
1½ tablespoons shortening
12 baby potatoes, parboiled
8 small onions, minced
3 carrots, pared and sliced
1 small garlic clove, minced
1 small onion, stuck with 3 cloves
⅛ teaspoon basil
3 tablespoons chili sauce
½ cup red wine
½ cup water

1) Lightly season the breast with salt. Lightly dust with flour.

2) Heat shortening in pan until bubbling. Place veal into shortening and saute over medium flame until browned.

3) Add the remaining ingredients, cover, and cook for approximately 1 hour or until veal is tender.

Serves 4

Veal Over Noodles

4 cups cooked veal roast, cut into thin strips
2 large onions, chopped
2 tablespoons butter
16 ounces canned spaghetti sauce
with mushrooms
12 ounces sour cream
cooked noodles with melted butter

1) Saute the onions in the butter until transparent. Add the veal and cook until lightly browned.

2) Add in the spaghetti and mushroom sauce. Simmer over low flame for 5 to 8 minutes.

3) Place sour cream in a bowl and add 2 cups of the hot veal, onion, and spaghetti sauce. Stir and return to pan. Heat over low flame. Pour over cooked and buttered noodles.

Serves 8

Baked Veal and Vegetables

6 pound breast of veal
⅓ pound salt pork, diced and rendered
10 small potatoes, peeled
10 small carrots
10 small onions, peeled
2 small rutabaga, peeled and cubed
1 large garlic clove, peeled
½ teaspoon salt
½ teaspoon pepper
1½ cups water
⅔ cup white wine

1) Render the salt pork in a hot pan and remove pork. Place the veal breast in the pork fat and brown on each side. Remove veal.

2) Brown the potatoes, carrots, onions, rutabaga, and garlic in the same pan. Sprinkle the bits of pork over the browned vegetables, and place the veal on top. Lightly season with salt and pepper, add the water and wine, cover and bake at 350 degrees for 2½ to 3 hours or until meat is tender.

Serves 6

Veal in a Cream Sauce

4 tablespoons butter
2 pound veal steak, untrimmed
dash of salt
dash of pepper
6 cups heavy cream

1) Lightly season the veal with salt and pepper. Place in a pan with melted butter and cook until lightly browned. Remove the veal and trim off the fat, discarding the bone. Cut into small cubes.

2) Place the remaining butter in the pan and cook the cubed veal once again until well browned. Add the cream and cook for 45 minutes or until veal is tender, stirring a few times while cooking.

Serves 4

Veal Stew

1 pound veal, cut into chunks
½ cup flour
2 slices bacon, diced
1 small onion, sliced
1 tablespoon oil
½ pound mushrooms
¼ teaspoon fresh thyme
dash of salt
¼ cup white wine
½ cup water

1) Dip the veal in the flour, coating thoroughly. Cook bacon in a Dutch oven over a medium flame. Remove bacon to paper towel, and brown the veal, one-half at a time, in the bacon drippings. Remove veal when browned.

2) In the same Dutch oven, cook the onions in the oil until the onions are transparent. Add mushrooms, thyme, and salt, and cook for 5 to 7 minutes. Stir in the white wine and the water, then add the browned veal.

3) Heat over high flame until the stew begins to boil. Reduce flame to a low setting and simmer for 1 to 1¼ hours, or until veal is tender. Break apart bacon, sprinkle the pieces over the stew and serve.

Serves 4

Breast of Veal with Cognac

2 pound breast of veal
1 teaspoon salt
½ teaspoon pepper
2 tablespoons butter
1½ tablespoons cognac, warm
⅓ pound sausage, chopped
8 white onions
1 small garlic clove, minced
⅓ cup water, boiling

1) Cut the veal into serving size pieces. Lightly season the veal with salt and pepper. Brown the seasoned veal in melted butter.

2) Pour flaming cognac over the veal. Add sausage, garlic, and onions. Cover and cook over a low flame for 30 minutes, stirring the juices often.

3) Drain the fat and add the boiling water. Cover and cook for 45 minutes to 1 hour.

Serves 4

Stuffed Veal Breast

4 pound veal breast
1 teaspoon salt
1½ pounds hamburger
2½ cups bread crumbs
1 large onion, chopped
2 tablespoons paprika

1) Slice a pocket in the veal breast. Rub the salt inside the pocket.

2) Mix the hamburger, bread crumbs, and onions, and stuff into the pocket. Close with toothpicks. Sprinkle the outside of the veal breast with the paprika.

3) Cover the veal breast with foil and place in a roasting pan in the oven at 350 degrees for 1¼ hours. Remove foil and bake for an additional hour, or until veal is rich and brown.

Serves 6

Breaded Veal in Red Wine

3 pounds veal cutlet, cut into 6 pieces
⅓ cup flour
pinch of salt
pinch of pepper
3 eggs, beaten
⅓ cup breadcrumbs
2 tablespoons butter
1 teaspoon thyme
2 bay leaves
1½ cups red wine

1) Mix the flour, salt, and pepper, and place in a plastic bag. Place each piece of veal in the bag and shake to season. Remove veal from bag and dip in eggs and then in breadcrumbs.

2) Cook breaded and seasoned pieces of veal over a high flame in butter until brown. Place pieces of browned veal in a casserole dish, add the thyme, bay leaves, and wine, and bake at 350 degrees for 35 to 40 minutes.

Serves 6

Veal and Mushroom Casserole

1½ pound ground veal
1 cup wild rice
3 cups water
1½ cup mushrooms
¾ cup celery, chopped
¾ cup onion, chopped
1 teaspoon Worcestershire sauce
½ teaspoon salt
1½ cans condensed cream of mushroom soup
⅓ cup sherry
⅓ cup Parmesan cheese, grated

1) Cook the rice in water, drain, and set aside.

2) Saute the veal until brown. Add the mushrooms, celery, onion, Worcestershire, and salt. Mix in the mushroom soup, sherry, and rice. Pour into a well-oiled casserole dish, sprinkle with cheese, and bake at 350 degrees for 1¼ hours.

Serves 6

NOTES

NOTES

NOTES

NOTES

NOTES

NOTES